# MUSHROOM

LIFE CYCLES

# BookLife
## PUBLISHING

©2021
**BookLife Publishing Ltd.**
**King's Lynn**
**Norfolk PE30 4LS**

A catalogue record for this book is available from the British Library.

**ISBN:** 978-1-83927-157-1

**Written by:**
Brenda McHale

**Edited by:**
Shalini Vallepur

**Designed by:**
Danielle Webster-Jones

Words that look like **this** can be found in the glossary on page 24.

# CONTENTS

# WHAT IS A LIFE CYCLE?

All animals, plants and humans go through different stages of their life as they grow and change. This is called a life cycle.

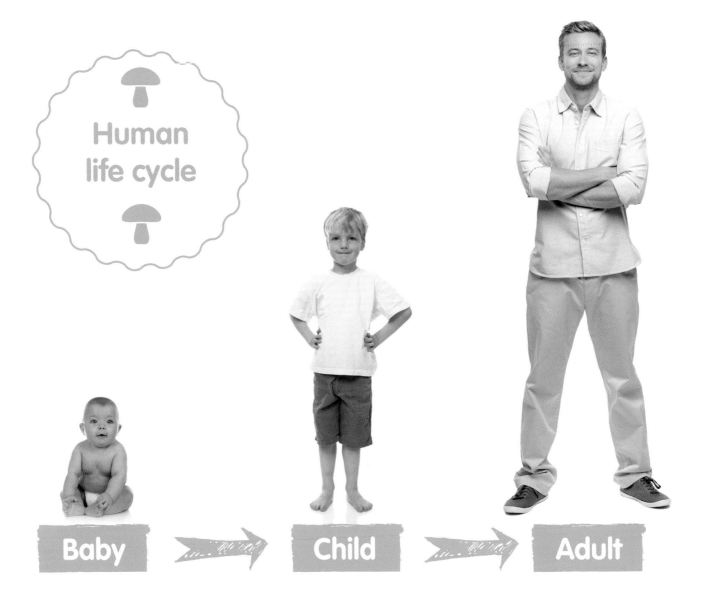

Human life cycle

Baby ➤ Child ➤ Adult

# WHAT IS A MUSHROOM?

A mushroom is a type of **fungus**. It is not a plant or animal. Mushrooms grow mostly underground. The part we see above ground is called the fruit body.

Some mushrooms are <u>poisonous</u>. Never touch mushrooms growing outside.

Cap

Gills

Stalk

# SPORES

New mushrooms grow from spores. Spores are made in the fruit body. They are too small to see.

Spores usually grow on the fruit body's gills.

Gills

**Spores get blown around by the wind.**

When they are ready, spores fall from the gills onto the ground.
Spores grow best in **shady** and **damp** places.

# UNDERGROUND

Most of the mushroom fungus grows underground. The spore grows lots of long threads that push down through the soil and join with other threads.

Threads

The threads make a big underground web called a mycelium. The mycelium grows in all directions underground and can get quite big.

There will be a mycelium in the soil underneath this mushroom.

# FEEDING AND GROWING

Mushrooms can't make their own food. Instead, they **absorb** their food through the mycelium from dead things in the ground. This breaks the dead things down into soil.

Soil is partly made from dead plants and animals that have been broken down.

These mushrooms will help the leaves break down.

**Mushrooms and other fungi are helping to rot this tree.**

Fruit bodies sometimes grow on dead and **rotten** trees. The mycelium feeds off the tree. This helps to break the tree down so that it isn't there forever.

# FRUIT BODIES

When the threads grow together, they start to grow into fruit bodies. The fruit bodies push up through the ground. This is the part of the mushroom that can be seen.

Mushrooms we buy from the supermarket are fruit bodies, too. They are grown in mushroom farms. Small ones are called button mushrooms.

The gills can be seen on bigger mushrooms.

# MUSHROOMS

Mushroom fruit bodies do not live for long. Sometimes they only last a day or two. The mycelium under the ground can live for hundreds of years.

These fruit bodies may only be around for a few days.

Mushrooms that are sold in supermarkets usually take around three weeks to grow and be picked. Sometimes it is longer. Farmers grow them in tunnels or big sheds.

**The mushrooms are kept cool and damp.**

# TYPES OF MUSHROOMS

Mushrooms come in lots of different shapes and sizes. Some are umbrella-shaped with the spores underneath the cap. Others are long.

How many different types of mushroom can you see?

Some mushrooms are brightly coloured to show that they are poisonous, but even brown or white mushrooms can be poisonous. Red mushrooms are sometimes called toadstools.

**Never touch mushrooms that you come across without asking an adult first.**

# MUSHROOM FACTS

Some animals eat mushrooms. Deer, rabbits, squirrels and slugs all love them. You might see nibbled mushrooms in the woods or in a garden.

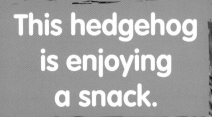

This hedgehog is enjoying a snack.

Sometimes the threads from a spore grow outwards in a ring.
When this happens, the fruit bodies make a fairy circle.

Fairy circle

# WORLD RECORD BREAKERS

## World's Biggest Growing Thing

The biggest growing thing in the world is a mushroom mycelium and all its fruit bodies. It is in Oregon, in the US, and is called the humongous fungus. It covers as much ground as a small town.

# Biggest Mushroom Cap

One of the biggest mushrooms that we can eat grows in countries in West Africa. The caps are usually bigger than 60 centimetres. The mushrooms grow in insect hills.

60

# LIFE CYCLE OF A MUSHROOM

**1** A spore drops from the fruit body and lands on the ground.

**2** It grows out long threads that join with threads from other spores.

**LIFE CYCLES**

**3** The threads grow a fruit body that pokes up through the soil.

**4** Spores grow in the fruit bodies until they are ready to fall.

# GET EXPLORING!

Why not take a walk in the woods or a park and see how many mushrooms you can find? Try looking in shady places. Remember not to touch any mushrooms you find.

# GLOSSARY

| | |
|---|---|
| **absorb** | to take in or soak up |
| **damp** | slightly wet |
| **fungus** | a living thing that often looks like a plant but has no flowers and lives on dead or decaying things |
| **gills** | thin flappy parts underneath a mushroom cap |
| **poisonous** | dangerous or deadly when eaten |
| **rotten** | dead and broken down |
| **shady** | when light has been blocked from an area |

# INDEX

## PHOTO CREDITS

All images are courtesy of Shutterstock.com, unless otherwise specified. With thanks to Getty Images, Thinkstock Photo and iStockphoto. Front cover & 1 – bergamont. 2 – Rubencress. 3 – valentinphotography, DutchScenery, Darren Pullman, fotokop. 4 – BesticonPark, Gelpi, Aila Images, Pete Pahham. 5 – Krasula. 6 – akslocum. 7 – Rastkobelic. 8 – Dmytro Ostapenko. 9 – ANURAK PONGPATIMET. 10 – oleg.z. 11 – Tonio_75. 12 – ArliftAtoz2205. 13 – Kelvin Wong. 14 – iwciagr. 15 – Videologia. 16 – Esther Purple. 17 – godi photo. 18 – Ondrej Prosicky. 19 – Matt Gibson. 20 – Qualit Design, marrishuanna. 21 – Migren art, Guppic. 22 – Erik Tanghe, Kichigin, OlegDoroshin, stocksolutions. 23 – LightField Studios.